HORSEPOWER

CHOPPERS

by Mandy R. Marx

Reading Consultant:
Barbara J. Fox
Reading Specialist
North Carolina State University

Capstone
press

Mankato, Minnesota

Blazers is published by Capstone Press,
151 Good Counsel Drive, P.O. Box 669, Mankato, Minnesota 56002.
www.capstonepress.com

Library of Congress Cataloging-in-Publication Data
Marx, Mandy R.
    Choppers / by Mandy R. Marx; reading consultant, Barbara J. Fox.
    p. cm.—(Blazers. Horsepower)
    Summary: Discusses motorcycle choppers, their main features, and how they
are built.—Provided by publisher.
    Includes bibliographical references and index.
    ISBN 0-7368-4388-4 (hardcover)
    ISBN 0-7368-6169-6 (softcover)
    1. Motorcycles—Customizing—Juvenile literature. 2. Home built
motorcycles—Juvenile literature. I. Fox, Barbara J.
    II. Title. III. Series.
    TL440.15.M37 2006
    629.28'775—dc22   2005000560

Credits

Jason Knudson, set designer; Patrick D. Dentinger, book designer;
    Kelly Garvin, photo researcher; Scott Thoms, photo editor

Photo Credits

Capstone Press/Karon Dubke, cover, 4–5, 6–7, 8, 8–9, 20–21, 28–29
Corbis/Kevin Fleming, 26–27; RF, 28–29 (background)
Getty Images Inc./David Paul Morris, 24–25; Kevin Winter, 12–13;
    Matthew Peyton, 16–17; White Cross Productions, 22–23
Heavy Metal Customs, 10–11
Ron Kimball Stock/Ron Kimball, 14–15, 18–19, 19

1 2 3 4 5 6 10 09 08 07 06 05

TABLE OF CONTENTS

ONE OF A KIND RIDE

A chopper is a motorcycle
built to personal taste. Just
like people, no two choppers
are the same.

Choppers are usually built from
scratch. Some people build their
own choppers. Others hire experts
to build bikes for them.

BLAZER FACT

The first choppers were made in the 1940s. They were called bobbers.

A custom paint job adds the finishing touch. Many chopper owners want a flashy paint job that attracts attention.

CHOPPER DESIGN

Choppers are built to go faster than most motorcycles. They are also meant to look like no other bike on the road.

Many choppers have lightweight frames. A lighter frame makes the bike quicker and easier to handle. Some chopper frames look like thin skeletons.

Choppers are built to look cool. A stretched-out front tire often sets a chopper apart from other motorcycles.

BLAZER FACT

If the front tire of a chopper is stretched out too far, the bike will tip.

PERSONAL TOUCHES

Custom bikes reflect the style of the owner. Many people like choppers better than regular motorcycles.

A paint job gives each chopper its own look. Some people paint their choppers to show their interests or beliefs.

BLAZER FACT

Choppers gained popularity in 1969, when the movie *Easy Rider* came out. Below is a copy of the bike from that movie.

CHOPPER DIAGRAM

Extended front tire

Kick stand

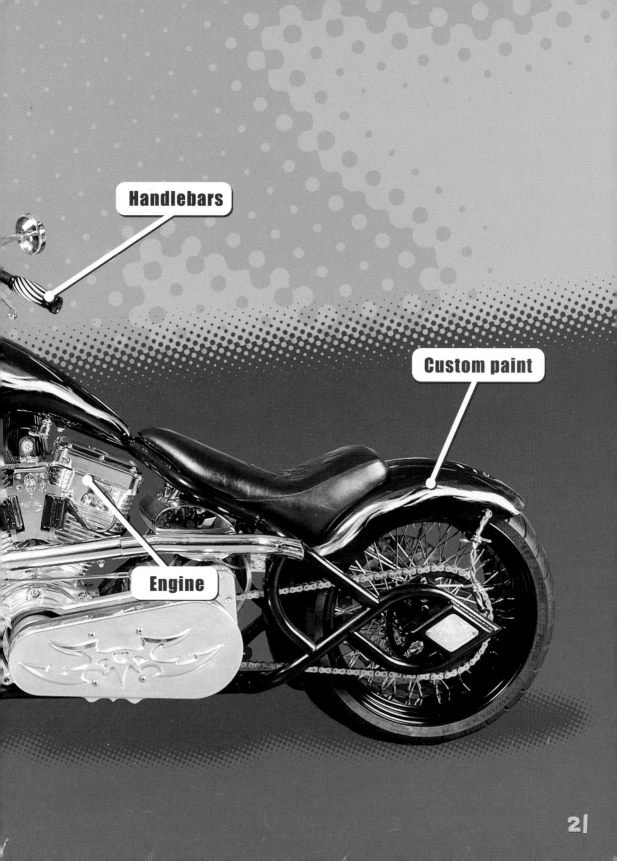

Handlebars

Custom paint

Engine

CHOPPERS IN ACTION

Choppers seem to fly
down the open road. Some
choppers can reach 120 miles
(193 kilometers) per hour.

23

Chopper owners share the thrill of riding. They join chopper clubs and hit the road together.

Chopper owners love to show off their bikes. They take them to motorcycle rallies around the world.

BLAZER FACT

J. C. "Pappy" Hoel held the first Sturgis Motorcycle Rally in South Dakota in 1938.

READY TO ROLL!